WAKE UP AND FEED YOUR MIND

TY'ASHIA JOHNSON

Copyright © 2021 by Ty'Ashia Johnson

All rights reserved. No part of this book may be reproduced or used in any manner without the written permission of the copyright owner except for the use of quotations in a book review.

ISBN: 978-0-578-33427-1

Scripture quotations are from The ESV® Bible (The Holy Bible, English Standard Version®), copyright © 2001 by Crossway, a publishing ministry of Good News Publishers. Used by permission. All rights reserved.

CONTENTS

Author's Note	v
INTRODUCTION	1
1. COMMUNICATION	3
Verbal Communication	3
Nonverbal Communication	5
Communication Styles	6
2. MENTAL HEALTH	8
Choose to Fight	11
Choose Joy	20
Choose Kindness and Love	22
Overcome Depression	26
3. FINANCIAL HEALTH	27
Leverage Your Time	28
Leverage Your Budget	30
Leverage Your Credit	30
4. ONLINE HEALTH	33
Avoid Comparing	34
Connect and Share	37
5. RELATIONAL HEALTH	39
Date Yourself	40
Make Real Friends	42
Date Others	46
6. MARITAL HEALTH	49
Honor, Don't Idolize	50
Ideal Marriage	52
Marriage Advice	54
Sex	64
7. OTHER THINGS WE SHOULD KNOW	71
Phone Etiquette	71
Handshakes	72
Conversational Etiquette	73

Old-Fashioned Manners	74
Professional Etiquette	75
8. POLITICAL HEALTH	79
9. NOTE TO SELF	82
References	87

AUTHOR'S NOTE

In the past couple of years, I've personally had to wake up and feed my mind to get myself out of a very dark hole. I had to awake from past mistakes, guilt, traumatic events, sorrow, pain, and even false happiness and put some of those things to rest. I use the word "awake" because I felt stuck. Without awakening, I would have never reached my full potential.

Feeding my own mind with the proper foundation has shaped me into the person I am today. By applying these principles, I overcame so much. The simple strength of these pieces of advice has been lost over the generations, so I had to share with the world how I became a better me—and how you can do the same. There were times when I felt I couldn't finish this book. Life threw everything at me at once. My mental health was already going downhill.

If I can't help myself, how can I help others? I wondered.

Then I reminded myself, *People do it every day.*

We help others when sometimes we can't help

ourselves, not realizing that that's a blessing in disguise. We actually *are* helping ourselves through this process. I had to reread my own book to pick myself back up when I needed clarity and wisdom in my life. I had to take my own advice.

Wow, I thought. *This is it. This is the beginning of something beautiful.*

I created this short book because less is sometimes more. We all have a story to tell, and we all have been through trials and tribulations, but when you wake up and see that life is a beautiful gift you only get once, you will appreciate everything that happens, no matter whether good or bad. When you feed your mind healthy and logical seeds, you will harvest fruitful plants. If you're in a dark place or you feel stuck like I did, read this book. It will help you wake up and become fed.

INTRODUCTION
WAKE UP AND FEED YOUR MIND

Eating a healthy, balanced diet improves your physical body, reduces body fat, or helps you gain weight the healthy way. We maintain a healthy diet by eating at certain times of the day, taking vitamins, replacing fried foods with baked foods, and a plethora of other habits. This usually results in a body that is refreshed, cleansed, and prepared to tackle life's challenges.

Just like we must feed our physical body, we must feed our minds. When we take account of what we feed our brain, we improve our communication and comprehensive health—mentally, financially, relationally, professionally, and politically.

So what do we feed our minds? Information! We should take account of our actions instead of allowing family, friends, or media to dictate our choices. This book is designed to guide young adults like you in almost every area that you can feed your mind.

Before you read the rest of this book, take a deep breath.

Inhale. One, two, three, four, five.
Now release that breath.
Exhale. One, two, three, four, five.
Now, clear your mind and relax.

Feed yourself good things and harvest wonderful fruits. Just like you give your body the nutrients it needs to thrive, your mind needs nutrition as well. It's time to wake up and feed your mind.

ONE
COMMUNICATION

Have you ever spoken with someone who seems to live behind a brick wall? Nothing gets through to them. Or perhaps they don't want to hear what you have to say.

Knowing how to communicate is essential in all areas of life. If you know how to communicate properly, you'll be better able to express yourself, won't endure as many misunderstandings, and will more easily connect with new people. Communication comprises both verbal and nonverbal aspects.

VERBAL COMMUNICATION

When communicating, how you speak (tone and body language) matters as much as what you say. The Bible talks about this. When I was speaking with a family member about a sensitive topic, my own tone caused miscommunication and confusion. I felt aggravated when I repeated myself several times and they still weren't understanding. My aggravation changed my tone drastically. I started yelling, and my aggressive body language heated things up, causing the other person to yell as well. If I had remained calm, paused, and come at the conversation from a different angle to uncover the misunderstanding, the situation could have had a better outcome.

Proverbs 16:24 says, "Gracious words are like a honeycomb, sweetness to the soul and health to the body."

Proverbs 15:1–2 says, "A soft answer turns away wrath, but a harsh word stirs up anger. The tongue of the wise commends knowledge, but the mouths of fools pour out folly."

An abrasive tone can prevent your recipient from hearing or understanding your meaning. If you come off as a jerk or even a know-it-all, people simply won't want to talk or listen to you. You may think you appear a different way than someone else perceives you. Be mindful of others with your words, tone, and intention when you talk with someone, especially if you're working with them to make a decision. If your discussion gets heated, ask yourself these questions:

- "How might this person misunderstand what I want to say?"
- "What words, tones, and gestures are not working to communicate my care and concerns clearly?"

The best tip is to follow James 1:19, which says, "Know this, my beloved brothers: let every person be quick to hear, slow to speak, slow to anger." Proverbs

17:28 also says, "Even a fool who keeps silent is considered wise; when he closes his lips, he is deemed intelligent." These verses give great examples of why verbal communication is important when practicing and learning conversation. If you're quick to hear and slow to speak, you give yourself the opportunity to properly respond, which most times prevents hurtful words or conflict. A fool is wise when he closes his lips because not everything needs a response, and knowing that is wisdom. If someone is talking with tension or stirring up an argument, why open your mouth to add fuel to the flames? In the heat of the moment, people say words they may not mean, and those are hard to take back. So being silent in heated times is the smarter route.

NONVERBAL COMMUNICATION

Communication comes in many forms, and any communication that doesn't involve language or verbal noises is considered nonverbal.

Gestures, body language, and facial expressions are all part of nonverbal communication. One time, a loved one started arguing with me. At that point in my life, I did not know how to properly communicate. When the person made an effort to sit down and apologize and talk things through, I crossed my arms, and my facial expressions told the person I did not care to listen. Without speaking, my body language spoke for me. Sadly, this caused an even bigger argument. Nonverbal communication plays a huge part in conversation.

Good communicators know how and when to listen. Everyone wants to be heard—that is the point of conversing—but when you know how to listen and think before speaking, you avoid a lot of unnecessary arguments and lasting hurtful words and actions in times of trouble.

COMMUNICATION STYLES

Your energy also rubs off on your friends, family, and significant others. If you yell at your children, then guess how they will communicate? This is called learned behavior. There are four types of communication styles: passive, passive aggressive, aggressive, and assertive.

Passive means you're more willing to please someone else while conversing than yourself. You are basically putting the other person first at the expense of your own communication needs.

Passive aggressive means you act apathetically toward everyone's needs, including your own, during conversation.

Aggressive means you focus only on your own needs while communicating. This isn't a productive communication style to have, because aggressive communicators don't care what comes out of their mouths, which leads to more conflict.

Assertive means you are careful to consider your needs and the needs of the other person. Caring about both parties shows you care as a whole, because you're listening and able to understand them and express yourself. If you apply all the correct forms of communication, you will master the art of properly conversing.

Everyone must stop and evaluate themselves sometimes. Improving your communication style may not be the easiest task, but you have to start somewhere. Don't lose a good relationship to avoid a hard conversation. We as humans were not put on the earth to be perfect. But we can better ourselves each and every day.

Feed your mind.

TWO
MENTAL HEALTH

So now we know what healthy communication looks like, but why does it even matter when we still feel this drained? What is going on with us emotionally, mentally, and physically?

And who are *we*? I'm talking about millennials and Generation Z.

Older generations sometimes say, "That's that young people stuff right there." They're talking about you and I. Your best friends, your colleagues, and perhaps your younger siblings. Maybe even your mom and dad. We are supposed to be the generations that change the world. Our generations have so much power. But we need one another's help.

Do you see how many millennials are depressed? Saddened? Do you see how many suicides there have been? Do you see how many of us feel alone? By chance, do you know of anyone in your life who is struggling with their mental health? Perhaps stress, depression, or loneliness? Some people make it look as if nothing is wrong while others broadcast exactly what they are going through. It's not too late—we still can help one another. Our window is now. But how can we tackle society's problems when we're struggling to achieve our own goals? When it's difficult to even get out of bed in the morning? I'm going to show you how.

We can do this. Together. Teamwork will help us improve our reality. But first, we must wake up and feed our minds. Let's get into this, shall we?

According to SingleCare's The Checkup, more than 264 million people suffer from depression worldwide. Women are nearly twice as likely as men to have depression (Fox 2018). Around 30 to 70 percent of suicide victims suffer from major depression or bipolar disorder (Mental Health America 2021). Reports of suicide attempts among college students increased from 0.7 percent to 1.8 percent from 2013 to 2018 (Ross 2019). Even so, ADAA.org says anxiety disorders are the most common mental health illness in the US, affecting 40 million adults ages eighteen and older or 18.1 percent of the population every year. That's a lot. Many things have caused an increase in depression and suicides among millennials. Some major causes are family history, serious medical illness, and drug and alcohol use. These are personal factors. Life events that can cause depression and suicide are financial problems, abusive relationships, loneliness or long-term isolation, expected and unexpected deaths, traumatic events, and work stress, among others. I discuss each of these issues throughout this book and provide solutions to these problems and causes. Overall, a good piece of advice would be to stop, breathe, and take one day at a time. Even though some things are uncontrollable, cope in the most healthy and positive ways possible and find peace within those situations. Especially ones you have no control over. Don't waste your life's moments stressing too much about things you don't control. This may sound harsh, but don't expect sympathy if you stay in broken situations. If you're in a bad situation, remember you've overcome previous obstacles and maybe even worse situations in the past and made it through. Don't let stress kill you. When you're in control, you have the power to remove yourself from unhealthy situations.

We all deserve to live a beautiful and healthy life. Life is not always glitter and gold, and we who make up society need to stop teaching each other and our children that life has to be sweet all the time. Chaos, sadness, and anger can be great motivators of change, so let's not seek to eliminate them, only balance them. It's all about learning how to balance life.

Sometimes, deep depression leads to despair and thoughts about taking your own life, but this is not the answer. I relate. Life can get really troubling and hard.

You may tell someone something personal, and they may try to hurt you with the information. Brokenness and betrayal sometimes results from sharing your struggles with the wrong people. They spread rumors about you, laugh at you, and you're left lonely. I've been there.

You may feel lost and alone, sometimes for prolonged periods. Take some personal time to address those feelings while remaining in community with others who care about you. What you decide to do next matters, because the same situations and feelings might reoccur. Meditate on and don't shy away from your problems when they happen the first time, and you'll be better prepared to deal with your emotions when they come back later. When obstacles come your way, they may seem disturbing, however, when you learn to push through situations, you'll be able to discover how strong you can be mentally, physically, and emotionally—on the inside and out.

But if I just listen to music or push my problems away, then I can escape!

In reality, the only true escape is overcoming your emotions and fears. Yes, life can be unfair, but your battle will not last forever, and you can only learn and move forward when you keep fighting. When obstacles come your way, they may seem disturbing, but later you'll discover they were for your own good. You can improve your mental health when you choose to fight, choose to have joy, and choose to act in kindness and love. Let's break our choices down.

CHOOSE TO FIGHT

Wearing a mask of false happiness while feeling dark and alone has to be one of the worst feelings you can experience. You feel like you have absolutely no one to talk to. You do have people in your corner you can trust, but you choose not to. I know I did.

Oftentimes we avoid dealing with our mental health simply because we don't want to be judged. We may even tell someone bits and pieces of what's wrong with us, but not the entire situation, because some things are hard to tell other people. At other times, we feel ashamed, scared, and too broken to even dare to share what's going on inside our brains.

With the anonymity of today's society, people can be cruel and evil.

I really can't trust anyone! you say.

I get it! People use your weaknesses against you for their own good, sometimes without knowing it. This can happen with anyone—your family, friends, coworkers, and intimate significant others. What a hurtful thing! It sucks the energy from us, we sink even lower, and we disconnect from our inner selves and the world.

Depression can significantly affect your everyday life and the way you act and go about your daily activities. It can affect your relationships with friends and family, your work, and your overall health. Your whole aura and demeanor can be negatively affected.

We all experience some form of depression throughout our lives. Some stages are more severe than others, but here's the good news: we can fight it. Everything you go through in life is a process. Everything we go through can be beaten. But you have to train yourself to persevere and develop tactics that will be a stronghold to you on your low days. When you start a new job, sport, or hobby, you begin at the bottom and have to train, learn, and grow in all areas. You won't become better than a beginner without working to gain knowledge and power, right?

The same applies to this concept. You have to train your mind to fight these battles and, most importantly, to know what to do when those challenges explode into your life. Sometimes you can anticipate bad things, but most of the time, life's challenges hit us unexpectedly and all at once. Allowing fear to choke you at these times can lead to chaos and ruin. So don't let fear stop you. You're stronger than that.

How do I train my mind to fight these battles?

Start small. When you begin a new gym workout, you don't lift 250 pounds unless you want to get hurt. If you have to start at five pounds, it's okay! Stop looking at what everyone else is doing and focus on your capabilities. We get so caught up in comparison, we lose ourselves.

Before a real workout, you have warm-ups. You need a similar warm-up for your emotional battles. Control your mind and find a healthy way to cope with your inner self. Many people—I'd say half the population—often misuse drugs, alcohol, or sex as coping mechanisms.

While a social drink or a puff or two might be okay, is it helping you solve your long-term problems? Or is it a temporary escape? If your "coping" mechanisms are preventing you from achieving your career, relationship, or other life goals, you're not coping!

Substances and bad habits may dull the pain of the moment, but are you learning to deal with pain? No. Using unhealthy coping mechanisms can hurt your mental and physical health in the short term and damage your life even more in the long run because you're avoiding necessary battles.

Here's an example. Let's say you get sad and depressed. It feels as if your life is in shambles, but when you drown your cares in alcohol, you feel calm and smooth with a clear head space. It feels good for the moment, but that's the key word.

Moment.

You become addicted to avoidance. And now you

can't stop. Now that you started drinking to cope, you slowly but surely become an alcoholic.

Now let's say the time comes for you to apply for a job. You may have all the necessary skills for that six-figure job you want, but now you can't keep the job because you have hangovers, you show up late, and you don't do quality work.

Get the point now?

Your frustration at work adds to your stress, and you lean into the alcohol. You beat the ones you love because the intoxication controls you. You lose friends because you drink too much at social gatherings.

But it's just a few drinks! you say.

Every habit starts somewhere. Everything you do in life is a choice. A repeated choice becomes a habit that can potentially control and affect your entire life.

It's okay to have fun! Love life! But your coping mechanisms are far worse managers of your life than you, I promise. Instead, learn to control your habits. Rein in your thoughts and change your way of thinking to address your problems head-on. That way, you can climb uphill and see the bigger picture from a bird's-eye view when you need to correct yourself. Don't compound your pain by avoiding it. Happiness and pain are both temporary. Fight through struggles. They may hurt now, but they will only fester if you ignore them. The joy of victory over your struggles is priceless. You can definitely pay for temporary happiness, but you can't pay for someone to give you endless joy. When you learn how to deal with your pain, even if the journey is long and lonely, you will be one step closer to success.

How do you cope with the pain in a healthy way, you ask?

Step one: Take care of your body! Exercising, eating healthy, and traveling are three great ways to do that.

EXERCISE AND EAT HEALTHY

Put your arms up! Stretch as high as you can.

This stretch feels good, right? I know. Exercising is one of the most important factors contributing to your health. Millennials are more likely to go to the gym and work out thanks to social media and its gym influencers. Jenn Sinrich explains in an Aaptiv.com article that with access to social media, you can find exercise inspiration on nearly every online platform. Even while scrolling through your feed during your breaks, you're inundated with information on ways to improve your physical wellness. People are buying cute gym clothes and are motivated by others' fitness goals, and they encourage the next person to go to the gym. When you exercise, it helps you stay healthy, take care of your body, and boost your mental health.

Exercising physically and mentally is better than taking pills and substances as an alternative. On social media, the lure of instant success is in so many advertisements for new weight-loss or weight-gain substances, and some ads promote supplements for staying fit. Some of these products may be legit, but most are not. Always talk to your doctor and do plenty of research before taking supplements that are not FDA approved.

Exercising gives you the ability to stay in shape whether you're trying to build muscle, bulk up, or slim down. It also benefits your overall health by reducing your risk of heart disease and improving your mood to minimize the effects of depression, stress, or anxiety. It can help your body manage blood sugar and insulin levels, too!

Exercise promotes better sleep and can even put a spark back into your sex life. Whether you're trying to reach a fitness goal or simply stay healthy, consult a trainer at a gym, find a free trainer on online platforms like YouTube, or, if you have extra funds, hire a personal trainer.

Be kind to your body. Trust me, it will pay off in the end.

Take initiative and start exercising! I don't mean just at the gym, but while we're on the topic, let's begin with physical exercise. Eating healthy and exercising play a major role in alleviating anxiety and depression, but working out physically does not always mean you're aiming to lose or gain weight. Working out has a lot of benefits for your mind as well. Going to the gym enables you to meet others and build a social life around physical activity, but you can also exercise at the park, around your neighborhood, or even at home.

Stop making excuses for yourself and find a way to do it! Working out is a major stress reducer, and it's an inexpensive and effective way to cope. Exercising releases a number of chemicals into your body, including norepinephrine, which can help regulate how you deal with stress and make your body more efficient. Norepinephrine is a hormone that mobilizes the brain and body for action. Exercising can also help relieve anxiety and has been a big part of many therapies for people suffering from anxiety disorders and depression. We all need endorphins.

The necessary counterpart to a healthy exercise routine is healthy fuel! You need a better relationship with food. Eat healthy and educate yourself on nutrition. Eating highly nutritious, balanced meals helps your mind function more effectively, and you will feel better internally and externally. You'll get better sleep, and you also won't feel so down all the time. Your diet plays a huge role in the way you feel. For example, if you sit around and eat fried foods and sweets all day, every day, you will always be tired. You won't feel good emotionally because you'll have low energy levels. The substances in those foods will affect how you think. Don't starve yourself and don't overeat unhealthy foods to look like someone else. Take care of your body.

If you're not ready to leap into an intense fitness program or meal plan, start small. Watch online videos, work out at home, cook a few inexpensive meals, and work your way up. Dedication requires daily practice, sacrifice, and discipline. Fuel and move your body while you are young so when you are older, you will have a healthy foundation to fight off harmful viruses or sicknesses. Keeping your immune system up-to-date and going to the doctor for regular checkups is responsible.

You can take easy steps to maintain a healthy immune system. Protect yourself from infectious diseases by practicing proper hygiene, getting vaccines and health screenings, and staying on top of medical research. As I touched upon in the introduction, eating healthy and exercising regularly is a good practice. Even with pandemics like the most recent COVID-19, maintaining a healthy immune system will give you an advantage when unexpected disease outbreaks occur. We never know when pandemics may come about, and even then, we still are always at risk for sickness, so it makes sense to maintain your health. COVID-19 taught people the importance of washing our hands correctly and not touching our bodies or faces with unclean hands. Dirty hands can cause infection. We should practice these things every day—not just when disease breaks out worldwide.

If seeing your progress will help motivate you, keep a journal to log your meals, heart rate, and exercises.

Feed your mind and your body.

TRAVELING

Imagine the sounds of the ocean, the waves crashing into each other, and the beautiful sunset. We all dream of being at the beach or exploring a different country, right?

Well, what could be better for our mental health?

Traveling the world has to be one of the most exciting things to think about, and it's not just about posting pictures. You get to go see new places, experience new cultures, learn their histories, try new foods, go on adventures, find new activities, and so much more! Traveling gives you memories that will last forever.

You can't get your time back. Social media, ironically, has encouraged more people to travel. The amazing views of other countries and different places around the US inspire our minds and make our adrenaline rush! Social media is a new lens through which to see the world, and with the tap of a finger, you get great ideas and options for where to visit next. Many of us have never even heard of some of the places we see online, even cities or states in our own country! Also, thanks to social media, millennials are traveling more than baby boomers (since millennials basically run the social media world).

The internet has also made it easier to travel. Unlike decades ago, you can now use apps to plan trips. You can book hotels and flights in packages to save money. You can rent houses for group trips. You can even plan activities to do abroad with the click of a button. All thanks to the digital world.

Traveling reduces stress. Have you ever told yourself you need a vacation? Well, yes. We aren't made to spend our entire lives working and sleeping. We all need a break, and a good vacation is the way to do it. Budget your money and save. Start a savings account and collect what you can here and there. Eventually, it will add up, and savings are important, especially when planning to travel. Learn more about budgeting in the Financial Health chapter.

Traveling boosts your mental health and state of mind. When you meet new people and get to adapt to new cultures, it helps with your personal growth. Sometimes we just need to disconnect from our daily life and experience new things. It's not good to keep doing the same things over and over again. Complacency is the devil's work, and when we get complacent, we get comfortable doing nothing. Then we wonder why we feel as if our life drags by without color and excitement! Dreaming about doing something and planning and putting in the work to do it are two totally different things.

Get in the habit of planning. Keep a journal or notebook and get busy! Travel guides and vacation planners are available to help you set up your perfect vacation. Do some research and plan your next trip, even if it's only the next city or state over. Seeing something new and going somewhere different allows you to open your mind and get out of your comfort zone. Some of us don't travel because we are simply too comfortable at home!

You mean to tell me that some of us have the time and money to go somewhere, but we don't? Wow.

Grab your friends or family members and go! Some people even learn a second language because they want to travel so much.

Millennials nowadays are even traveling alone. If you want to travel alone, for your safety, stay updated on what is going on in the world and keep up with the news and important world events. Anything can happen anywhere and anytime, so have some knowledge about where you are going and what is going on there.

Traveling alone is basically taking yourself on a nice, extended date. You get to go on all the adventures you want. You get to try new foods and explore new places, and you even have the chance to talk to and meet new people wherever you are. A lot of people find romance and meet lifelong friends when traveling alone. According to the website Solo Traveler, in 2019, a third of Generation Z said they prefer to be alone when traveling, and almost 20 percent said they want to take a solo backpacking trip or gap year. Find yourself and be free. If you have low self-confidence, this will boost it. You'd be surprised how much traveling (even alone!) can do for you. Wake up and feed your mind.

CHOOSE JOY

Whoever you are, you deserve joy, not just happiness. Happiness is temporary. Joy is eternal. You can have joy and be completely happy, but you can't truly be happy without joy. Joy uplifts the soul. It comes from within. Happiness is a temporary emotion based on your current situation, financial security, mental health, emotional state, and more. Joy is the belief that all your struggles will be worth the fight, and it shines on the outside regardless of your circumstances. Proverbs 17:22 says, "A joyful heart is good medicine, but a crushed spirit dries up the bones." Choose to be joyful. You deserve every moment.

If you are struggling with suicidal thoughts or actions, know this: suicide doesn't end your pain. It ends your life, and that's not what you really want, I promise. Take it from someone who has been there personally. Fight through those feelings, because they are temporary, and you can and will outlast them. Choosing joy is not always an easy fight. It is definitely not an overnight process. Challenge yourself to be better, overcome your thoughts, and get the help you need. Your clashing pain, emotion, and sadness is trying to overwhelm your life. It's a terrible feeling, I know.

But if everything in life was easy to get through, it wouldn't be fun. Ugh, imagine the tedium! Life without struggle would be bland. How would you know how to help the next person if you never go through hard times? How would you give your friends, family, and children advice and wisdom if you never have a story to tell them? Going through struggles and pain help make you stronger and give your life meaning. This is the way we should all see it.

We all have different outlooks on life, but our beliefs affect our actions, and our actions determine the outcomes.

When we are all facing hard times, no one wants to hear the cliché saying "everything will be okay." But it will!

I live by the saying "timing is everything." Since I started applying those three words to my life, my perspective changed for the better. It is okay to wait things out. Never rush. Acknowledge that you don't know everything. Be open-minded and willing to gain knowledge and wisdom no matter your age. Proverbs 19:20 says, "Listen to advice and accept instruction, that you may gain wisdom in the future." Depression is a scary place. Once you fall in, it can be extremely hard to get out. Nothing worth fighting for comes easily. You are worth the fight. Always remember that.

CHOOSE KINDNESS AND LOVE

Attack your problems with a mental workout called *kindness*. That little skull of ours does more than you think! In my opinion, this exercise is crucial. Everything affects your mental state, so why not take care of it to the best of your ability?

A step-by-step workout for mental kindness can be as easy as meditating and speaking kind words. For example, you could tell yourself, "May I be happy and accept myself the way I am. May I be filled with joy and abundance." Speak positively, stop, and inhale and exhale. This can all be a two-minute, completely free process. Feed and rest your mind.

Have you ever noticed that people with all the money in the world, people who have the "perfect" bodies and faces and lives, are some of the most depressed people on this planet? Have you ever wondered why so many famous and well-known individuals attempt suicide or end up going to a rehabilitation center?

Depression and anxiety often look "normal."

A depressed person doesn't have to be grumpy and lie in bed all day. An anxious person doesn't have to walk around carrying or showing loads of anger or sadness. Depression can look like a pot of gold. And that's the scary part. Depression doesn't have a "look."

Even suicidal thoughts and actions can go undetected.

"I never knew," grieving loved ones say.

"She didn't seem like that type of person," friends say.

"She was the funniest and most energetic person I've ever known," others say.

Always love deeply and actively seek to support others' emotional health. Just because a person is always laughing and smiling does not mean they feel it inside. By spreading more genuine love around, you can make the world a much better place.

Ask people how they are doing and show interest in the answer.

Give a stranger a compliment.

Go out of your way to help someone or call someone you haven't talked to in ages.

You know the saying "one man can change the world"? Well, it's true. All it takes is one person. One single person. The smallest gesture can go a long way. The world has always been filled with loving, caring, and genuine people.

People sometimes say mean things because they feel picked on or insecure. We cannot justify picking on other people. What is the point? What do you get out of being hurtful?

Does it pay your bills?

Does it foster healthy relationships?

Does it get you promoted in your career?

Does it make you feel better?

Life has a sense of humor, and the person you're picking on could be you in the blink of an eye. Spread love, because life can humble you real quick. For the price of zero dollars, we can all help one another by doing small acts of kindness. With social media, you can even do great acts of kindness and make a person's day from miles away. Be a trustworthy person someone can talk to so you can receive the same in return. You get what you give in this world.

We will all need a great support system many times throughout our life. We all need someone we can trust, and those people are hard to come by these days.

Strive to be a great friend and a great listener. Sometimes all people want is to be heard. Imagine helping someone out in many ways or saving a life all because you were there to listen to them. Recognize your own social needs and make time for other people.

Love other people, and you'll learn how to better love yourself.

When you feel good, make someone else feel good. Always remain humble. Create a healthy environment for yourself. Negative environments and negative people shift your attitude, daily performance, and overall health in the same direction: down.

Commitment to love and creating a positive

environment is what you need. But we have to make the best out of every situation, right? If negative people surround you, step up, be brave, and light the room with your love and joy. Why be scared? Why allow nerves to prevent you from being a good person when others around you aren't?

Eventually, others will either follow your lead and pick up those good traits, or you'll lose those people or choose to (rightly) leave that environment. If your friends or family gossip about or do wrong to others, remove yourself from the situation. Even though you might not be saying or doing those things, sticking around will hurt you.

A friend should never pressure you to hurt others or to create a toxic environment.

When you make kindness a habit, you take your mental exercise one step further and create a healthy environment for yourself and others. Remove yourself from tough situations to avoid negativity. When you have success with that, show others how to do the same. We all have certain things we want to achieve in life. Set goals and stick to them. Focus on those accomplishments.

People always pay attention to what you do and say, so aim to be the kind of person that demonstrates good habits. Ultimate love involves leadership. Even if we don't know where it may take us, we can lead the people who look up to us to a positive environment that fosters personal growth. Create your own habitat for others to see that it's okay to step out of your comfort zone. While helping others, you're also helping yourself. Choose to act in love and kindness today, because you may not get the chance tomorrow. People will always remember how you made them feel far more than what you did for them.

OVERCOME DEPRESSION

An idle mind is the devil's playground. When you seclude yourself from the world, your mind gets trapped in so many different loopholes, waiting for sadness to ferment into depression inside your mind.

So take action and put your mental health first. If you don't like your job because the negative energy there affects your mental state, find another one. Hanging around draining people? Find positive friends. Tired of being depressed all the time? Change your environment and try a different approach to find happiness and joy. You are in control of you, and you have the power to change your situation for yourself and your loved ones.

Life brings its challenges. Fight through them. Make time your best friend by spending it well.

Feed your mind.

THREE
FINANCIAL HEALTH

Let's talk about money! Dollars, coins, or plastic—oh, how we all love money. We need it to live, right? Not everyone always spends a lot of money. A lot of people like to save. And some of us are the complete opposite.

In 1 Timothy 6:10, the Bible says, "For the love of money is a root of all kinds of evils."

When you love money, you will do anything to keep it and get more of it. If the opportunity arises, you may do things you never imagined only to gain money, which could lead to life-changing consequences.

Instead, focus on and enjoy the way you are able to make your money (yes, that means work!) and what you are blessed to do with it—whether that means going on a nice vacation, donating to someone in need, or creating more revenue to achieve your goals.

We all want an easy life, but few of us understand exactly how much hard work and dedication it takes to get there. The entrepreneurial mindset is common.

But an entrepreneur's life comes with unique struggles that people don't talk about.

Let me tell you a secret: most rich people do what is hard and tedious. That is why they have "easy" lives. Consistently poor people do what is quick and easy, and that's why their lives are much harder.

We look at wealthy individuals and think the life they have is worth more than ours. We look at the nice handbags, watches, cars, mansions, and extravagant vacations, and we want all those things. Who wouldn't? But we don't see all the hard work, long nights, battles with mental health, or repeat failures it took to gain that wealth. All we see is the highlights. Being wealthy is not the ultimate goal even though society (in many cases) makes it so.

You have to hustle for the lifestyle you wish to have.

Hustling does *not* mean working all the time. Your body needs rest as well. Your mind needs rest. Hustling means leveraging your time and resources well while working hard for the things you want.

Leverage means identifying and doing the least costly action that will yield the largest, most beneficial result. Once you do that, you only need faith the size of a mustard seed.

In Matthew 17:20, Jesus says, "For truly, I say to you, if you have faith like a grain of mustard seed, you will say to this mountain, 'Move from here to there,' and it will move, and nothing will be impossible for you."

LEVERAGE YOUR TIME

Time leverage is probably the most fundamental technique you need when striving for financial success. No matter how beautiful, smart, or driven we are, we all have the same amount of time in a day: twenty-four hours. Devise a strategy to leverage your time. A person can work their butt off to accomplish their life goals, but that still doesn't necessarily mean that they used their time efficiently.

This generation thinks life is all about work, work, work. But what happens when you work so much that you sacrifice other important aspects of your life? What is your time really worth, and how can you spend it to maximize what is important to you?

What happens when you want to open your own business? You have the money because you devoted every possible waking hour to work, but you don't have time to plan it all out, think it through, structure how and what you want or need, or build and maintain a good team. This is why hustling does not mean working 24-7. You need to leverage your time and know the importance of it. You can of course pay someone to do work for you to start whatever business venture you choose, but will you have the time to go to the meetings? Will you have time to think everything through and make informed decisions? Probably not. You will lose sleep sometimes with any job, but don't make it a recurring habit.

What you do with your time (and your money) is more important than what you make.

Remember that time is everything with making money, building credit, starting a business, going to college, and managing finances as a whole. Millennials are often told that they can do it all, but the real key to financial success is learning to spend your time on what matters most.

LEVERAGE YOUR BUDGET

Knowing about finances isn't worth much if you don't take steps to meet your goals. Budgeting is important, especially when saving money. Everyone should have a budget of some sort. It helps you control your spending habits, track your day-to-day expenses, save money, and take charge of your overall finances.

According to Dave Ramsey, the first steps to start budgeting are 1) writing down your total income, 2) listing your expenses, 3) subtracting your expenses from your income to equal zero, and 4) tracking your spending. Budgeting takes consistency and perseverance and, of course, time. Change your desire into a desire for change, and then do it. Once you get the technique down and learn how to budget, you'll soon see extra money in your pockets and savings.

Money management is a major key to saving and learning financial freedom.

Pay your tithes, because if you don't, you are robbing yourself. God can't bless you with opportunities to give if you only ever take. You are cursed when you don't pay your tithes.

LEVERAGE YOUR CREDIT

Financial literacy classes can teach the basics of money management: budgeting, saving, investing, giving, and using debt. This knowledge lays the foundation for building strong money habits early on and avoiding many of the mistakes that lead to lifelong money struggles. Let's start with two of the most basic finance terms describing debt.

Principal is the money you originally agree to pay

back. When you take out a $3,000 loan, the principal is $3,000. If you plan to pay more than your monthly payment amount, which is the smartest thing to do, you can request the lender or servicer apply the additional amount immediately to the loan principal.

Interest is the fee a lender charges a borrower for the use of borrowed money. Here's an example. Interest is usually expressed as an annual percentage of the principal. The rate is dependent upon the time and value of the money, the credit risk of the borrower, and the inflation rate. The interest rate, expressed as a percentage, is the interest per year divided by the principal amount.

For example, if I give you $100 and you want to give it back in five days, I might charge you $0.50 per day to borrow this money. I can't use it since I'm lending it to you and would like compensation for my loss of use. So at the end of five days, you give me back $102.50 because the $100 (principal) you borrowed plus $0.50 (interest) over five days equals $102.50.

Now let's talk about credit literacy. Credit literacy equips us with the knowledge and skills we need to manage our money. Basically, credit is king. Your credit represents how responsible you are.

When you apply for a loan for a house, a car, or anything else, you can have money in the bank, but if you never pay your bills on time, then your credit shows lenders how irresponsible you are.

If you don't make a lot of money but you pay your bills on time, your credit shows you are responsible and trustworthy enough to pay back the loan on whatever you are trying to purchase. When you pay your bills on time, you are likely to have a better credit score.

When you don't make payments on time, it's the opposite. You also get charged late fees that can accumulate interest and build up over time. Today, credit is almost worth more than your money, though you can still bypass some credit restrictions with enough in savings or by paying for purchases in full.

Another important factor of your credit is credit history. Credit history is a record of how you repay debts and your demonstrated responsibility in repaying debt. It is the main component of your credit reports and a big influence on your credit. Interest rates affect your credit as well. Credit literacy is a crucial skill to have for your future and the future of your family.

Talk to a credit advisor or someone you can trust that has knowledge and experience in building and maintaining a good credit score. Inform yourself about credit and good financial practices and start building your future today.

Feed your mind.

FOUR
ONLINE HEALTH

Love it or hate it, social media is a reality of our modern time. Are you taking the perfect pic for the 'gram because you feel handsome or beautiful and want to share a cool memory or a cute photo with the world? Or is it because you want likes and validation to fit in with the rest of society?

For many people, the second answer is truer. Maintaining a social media presence has become one of the most phenomenal demands on millennials and Generation Z. In fact, social media has caused a ton of modern ethical dilemmas. So many things have changed over the past few decades because of social media and technology itself.

How exactly has social media changed technology? The most profound things that have changed are expectations, intimacy, communication speed, and fashion, all over the past couple of decades. *Social* media? How about *unsocial* media? I'd say lack of love and education has driven this generation to social media and made it become so deflated. We experience too much fake, not enough real. Too many bodies, not enough souls. Too many sounds, not enough laughs. Too many hearts, not enough love. Too many words, not enough kindness.

Social media is and most likely will be a game changer for decades to come. It already has been so far. Social media is a great way to find any resource you can bring to mind. Using it can generate income, help you keep in touch with old friends, and much more.

But the dark side of social media is making us asocial. The bullying, the fake lifestyles, the chaos that social media can cause with a quick scroll or comment? We have to fix this. We should want to help make this world a better place, and by the looks of it, we're only making it worse in a lot of different ways, specifically by first not taking care of ourselves.

Technology has definitely changed the communication game. Nothing is the same because of it. Communication technology has connected the world but flooded us with more information than we can ever possibly digest—and we must weigh the pros and cons.

AVOID COMPARING

Have you ever found yourself scrolling for hours upon hours? Have you ever woken up with so many important things to do, and yet the first thing you jump to is browsing social media? Have you ever hated yourself, your body, your hair, or even your life and career all because you want to look like and do what the influencers do? This behavior is unhealthy for you and everyone around you.

Social media has contributed to depression,

suicide, and unhealthy mindsets in millennials and the younger generations. You can easily look at a handful of people's lives on social media and think you are not doing enough, all because you're not on this level or that level yet or because you don't have enough money or look a certain way.

Paradise isn't always what it seems, but sometimes you have to go there to know that. Do not be dismayed by what you see online, because half the time, what you see isn't reality.

But why is it so easy to base your real life on someone else's internet life? Just like your body, your mind must consume a healthy diet as well. Be careful of what you feed it. Feed your mind positivity, nourish it with education, and plant good seeds so you may have a positive day, a positive life, and reap good productivity. This growing process of maturity can take time. Spending your entire life on social media is a learned behavior.

If you wake up and scroll through social media first thing, what are you looking at? Does the content enrich or detract from your life? Does it plant good seeds or bad? You want to stimulate your mind every day, and whatever you plant grows. When you sow, you want to reap good things. In 2 Corinthians 9:6, Paul says, "The point is this: whoever sows sparingly will also reap sparingly, and whoever sows bountifully will also reap bountifully." Similarly, Proverbs 11:18 reads, "The wicked earns deceptive wages, but one who sows righteousness gets a sure reward."

Wake up and read the Bible, listen to a podcast, exercise, clean up around the house, or get other things done. Start your day off right and end your night positively as well. Usually when we get ready for bed, our thoughts wander to negative places. Imagine having an amazing day, and you lie down in bed for a couple hours and scroll through social media. Soon you grow envious or lose self-confidence because your day doesn't look as incredible as the next person's. The next thing you know, the devil is whispering in your ear that you're not good enough. Now you can't sleep because you're sad and anxious.

You cry yourself to sleep, only to wake up in the morning worried about your thoughts from last night. So you get back on social media while lying in bed, just to get sad all over again and start your day off wrong. See how easily that happens? Then it becomes a cycle.

Social media use can be our own personal butterfly effect, trapping us in the habit of comparison that leads to catastrophic results. We must limit our time on social media and use our limited time to learn, grow, and support rather than compare. Protect your self-worth.

I'll give a couple more examples.

Say you have a huge accomplishment you need and want to finish. You're so excited to start your new project. You have the right mindset and you're motivated and ready to go. A couple of days turn into weeks and those weeks turn into months. Where did the time go, and what did you do with your time?

Social media is addictive. The average time a person spends on social media is interesting. An article by Nick Galov on Review42.com says, "People spend on average two hours and twenty-two minutes on social media every day." Social media has such a huge effect on every individual's brain. Statistics have shown that excessive social media use results in a dramatic shift in behaviors, attitudes, and lifestyles, especially for millennials.

This does not mean being on social media is only negative, but we have to talk about it to help each other have a healthy social media mindset.

Misuse of social media has ruined relationships and friendships. So many of us compare the next person's life to our own. We call them "role models" based on what they put online.

But do we know what goes on behind the closed doors of another person's life? Do we know the struggles they may face on a daily basis? Or do we look at a post or profile and expect our real life to be like theirs?

We expect what we see on our cell phones to become our own personal reality. Make a point to discuss this with your friends and potential or current significant other. If you or the people you care about are so caught up in the social media world that you lose touch with reality, your relationships could become as shallow as what you see on the screen, and you may lose genuine connection.

Don't let social media control how you think your individual life or relationships should be.

CONNECT AND SHARE

Social media does have many pros. For instance, it is a good way to keep in touch with relatives and colleagues that live near and far and even stay informed on important events around the world. Many people use social media as a platform to give advice and allow themselves to spread and receive positivity. Platforms like Google Podcasts and YouTube are in high demand, and people use many great channels like these to reach out and help others. Social media has created a new industry and enabled companies and freelancers to make money. You can see different parts of the world with a click, read a book virtually, and so much more.

Overall, you should use social media to enrich your relationships rather than detract from them. Be smart about how you use your time.

Feed your mind.

FIVE
RELATIONAL HEALTH

Before you can be a good friend or significant other, you have to learn to love yourself. Find yourself, and the rest shall follow. We all think we want to be popular or well respected. We all want hundreds of likes on our pictures, and we all want to feel loved and look important, right?

Why? To impress other people? If you live your life trying to prove a point to others, you will always be disappointed. You were not created to live for someone else. You were not born to impress the next person or put on fake personas. You are you, so be you with pride.

Discernment is the ability to judge well, and it's often an underdeveloped skill. Before deciding to say or do something, make sure you have as much information as possible.

We often end up hurting ourselves by jumping into intimate relationships and friendships without adequately understanding the consequences of our decisions. But constantly grasping for love from other people hurts them—and you!

Learn to love yourself fully first, because you shouldn't need someone to make you feel happy. While we all need support at times, happiness is your choice. Make yourself happy and let others add to your happiness at the right time. Don't force a relationship or friendship when you feel empty, because depending on someone else to make you happy only leads to ruin. Take care of yourself—heart, mind, and soul—and you'll have healthier relationships too.

So how do we do it? Read on!

DATE YOURSELF

If I could do my relational life all over again, I would. I'm sure a lot of us would. We preach loving yourself first, but we fail to live it out and don't understand the meaning behind what we say. Understanding is the beginning of knowledge.

Here's why you should date yourself. Knowing yourself is one thing, but understanding yourself is far harder. With time, you will learn more about what you want. When you date yourself, you give yourself time to grow and learn. It's fun!

Go to the movies by yourself. Take yourself out to eat. Find a new hobby.

It may seem a bit odd at first, but I promise, the more you do it, the more you'll enjoy it and appreciate the time to reflect and learn about who you are. Going on dates with yourself is normal. A lot of people do it, but until I took the time to see for myself, I was unaware of the joy it brings. I learned so much more about what I need and want.

Society makes us feel like we are incomplete without a boyfriend or girlfriend or best friend for every outing. No! Jump out there and forget what the world thinks you should do. Live for you. Continue to date yourself even if you are in a relationship. The older you get, the more you change, so use this time to get reacquainted with who you are today! Change is good, but expected change is better.

If you don't have confidence, take the time to date yourself, trying new fashions or new hobbies without worrying about judgment. Create your own personal space while single or unmarried. Confidence gives you the ability to be comfortable in your own skin. It allows you to own every situation you encounter. If you constantly need a companion, dating yourself will help you get more comfortable with your own company. This independence will help your next intimate relationship be balanced and not codependent.

You invite problems by not dating yourself before you get into an intimate relationship. When you are so used to being with your significant other or around friends, you can't function without that company and comfort. While this isn't a bad thing, what happens when you go through a breakup or a friend moves out of town? It's easy to get depressed because of loneliness.

A lot of millennials aren't used to being alone. Being confidently alone isn't praised or accepted enough. It's not healthy to always feel the need to be surrounded by others. When you master the art of being alone—spending a day without texts or calls, going out alone, and depending on yourself—you might crave your own personal space more often.

I encounter so many people who have separation anxiety. Separation anxiety in adults is when someone is afraid of being separated from a person, people, or even pets. Changes in your environment such as a new house, school, friendship, or relationship can trigger this disorder.

Say, for example, you have always been in a relationship and you never date yourself or give yourself any recognition. You always consider yourself—consciously or unconsciously—subordinate to your significant other or friend. You eventually become a little annoyed with being tied up, but if you break up or go away on a vacation, you can get separation anxiety.

Dating yourself takes self-discipline when first learning, but every individual can learn this habit. It is never too late to recognize and meet your own needs.

Even living alone can give you a sense of independence if you're in a position to do so. If not, that's okay. It's up to you to find the time to love yourself as a whole. Imagine waking up and buying yourself flowers or a new video game. Imagine being so in love with yourself that you can recognize and deflect negative energy—all because you took the time to learn about yourself.

Taking this step will give you the freedom you need to find yourself. You deserve to fall in love with yourself daily.

MAKE REAL FRIENDS

When you know who you are and what you need, you can more easily make real friends. Friendships are beautiful. You go through times of joy and work through disagreements. You share your deepest secrets, memories, and most of all, love. Finding and keeping a quality friendship is as hard as finding and keeping a good intimate relationship. Both types of relationships need to be maintained.

Polish your friendships, and you'll be able to polish yourself as well.

You will cherish a true friendship forever. Many of us have the same best friends from our childhood, high school, or college. Some of us will meet new friends or best friends as we learn and grow. Some of us will lose people along the way.

Friendships, by their nature, require trust. Without caution, people will be hurt. Friends betray each other and set one another up. Friends turn into frenemies. This is heartbreaking and needs to be changed.

My parents told me, "You'll only meet about two or three real friends in your lifetime." This is true. Not everyone is supposed to be your longtime friend, but that does not mean they have to be an enemy. Friends and acquaintances should have distinct levels of intimacy. An example of an acquaintance is someone you used to go to school with or passed every day at work, but you don't keep in contact with them on a regular basis.

You can trust a real and true friend with nearly anything. They respect you and your moral values. They uplift you and support your dreams and aspirations, and they're honest and hold you accountable.

A fake or toxic friend puts you down, doesn't support you, and tells you what other people say about you. And you have to ask yourself, "Why are they so comfortable talking negatively about me to my other friends?" A fake friend is never truly happy for you, is disrespectful, makes you the butt of jokes, gossips a lot, and constantly tries to one-up you.

Who in your life has these qualities? Sit down and decide who is real and who is fake, who is a friend and who is an acquaintance. Fake friends can negatively impact your life. Sometimes friendships do expire, just like relationships, and that is perfectly okay. Not everybody in your life is meant to go through the next chapter with you. But, if you notice, the real and true people are going to commit and will be there always. You won't have many of them, and that's a good thing.

You don't need to tell every "friend" or acquaintance about your next move or what's going on in your life. Take precautions when sharing information. Not everyone is happy for you, and not everyone needs to know your business all the time. This includes family. Some things are meant for only you to know. You become more like the people you hang around. If you don't want to be known as a person who speaks negatively or does bad things or dresses a certain way, then don't spend time with people who do. Yes, small things like presentation, association, and representation matter. Never say or think you can't or won't end up doing the things your friends do. Your friends have a big influence on you, so avoid doing things solely to fit in.

Today, people can meet new friends and acquaintances online, which is great! Genuine connection on social media can be beneficial, but people often avoid personal connection in favor of "clout" and use likes and followers to make their way to the top. Don't be fooled by others' online personas. Surround yourself with people with good energy who encourage you to become a better person.

We all have dreams we want to accomplish in life, right? Most of the time, I choose to hang around people who are wiser and older, people who have much more than me. Why? Because it inspires me to do better, to want more out of life, and to accomplish the things I want. They push me to be a better me. You can push yourself only so far—but real friends can push you farther.

Now look at the damage fake friends can have. If you surround yourself with those who want nothing out of life, watch TV or scroll through social media all the time, or always drag you down, you will soon pick up those energies and habits and do the same.

What happened to me? you'll eventually find yourself asking. *I was starting to do good for myself, and now look.*

No, this is not the way things should be. If you do have a friend or friends who only talk about their dreams and sit around all day, help them out. Give them advice on what they could be doing to be more productive and make their dreams reality. A true friend wants to see others succeed. They don't even have to be someone you know. The best advice I've gotten came from complete strangers. Start talking to people and pursue meaningful conversations. When someone gives you advice, take heed. When you can give advice, give. If you have the knowledge and wisdom to help someone else out, whether big or small, don't be scared to offer your expertise.

Sometimes we want to see someone do good—but not better—than us.

Read that again.

Some people will only give a certain amount of advice, none at all, or even purposely give you the wrong advice. Fake friends will see you falling and not offer a helping hand. Although you shouldn't depend on one person for everything, if a "friend" consistently refuses to help others, they aren't the friend for you.

Even you could be this type of person, so ask yourself these questions to find out:

- Do you feel more confident when your friends are worse off?
- Are you jealous when your friends or family succeed?

If the answers are yes, you should address the root issues of this behavior so you can be more confident and be a better friend. If you've ever found yourself unsettled because a friend is in a "better" position than you are, choose instead to be happy for them so you won't steal your own happiness. Don't let jealousy (which comes from insecurity) or spite make you lose a good relationship. Choose to be happy for other people, especially those you are close to. Your time will come.

Society has pushed millennials to believe life is a race. Time is a precious thing, but it always moves forward. Don't spend yours bringing someone else down or withholding help from those who need it. You get what you give in this world, and whether you are up or down, you will always need a left or right. We all have room to win. Sometimes you may feel like everyone around you is winning while you endure failure and heartbreak. Look instead at how far you've come and help others do the same.

DATE OTHERS

Once you know how to date yourself and make real friends, you might be ready for a romantic relationship. A relationship can be challenging, like most things in life. Love is the most powerful thing in the world and can make you do crazy things if you allow it to. "Above all," 1 Peter 4:8 says, "keep loving one another earnestly, since love covers a multitude of sins."

When you first fall in love, your whole life stops. We all go through the emotional, hormonal rollercoaster. At some points, it's the best feeling in the world, and at others, it's the worst feeling known to man. But perfect love, perfect people, and perfect relationships don't exist, and neither does a perfect you. So don't expect one. Simply strive to become the best version of yourself every day.

Dating as a millennial is tough and confusing. To a certain extent, social media, the internet, music, and the opinions of others teach us what a relationship is and should be. And people are following that advice!

Social media lies often. Be careful of the content you're consuming. Some people want to be players—they want a lot of men or women and consider it a conquest when they "hit this" or "hit that." Some people don't even understand what love or relationships should look like, and how would they? All the memes, hashtags, and inspirational quotes are feeding them false information.

"You will fall in love with three people in your life," goes the old saying, "and the third one is the one for you." An old wives' tale. Whoever and whatever relationship you are meant to have will find its way to you, no matter how long it takes. We all date people and don't end up marrying them, and that is okay. Playing with someone's emotions on purpose, however, is not okay. This is how people get hurt. Purposely toying with someone's feelings is fake love, and recognizing this requires discernment. When people show you who they are the first time, believe them. People can change only if and when they want to.

We oftentimes stay in relationships because of a history with them, emotional attachments, soul ties, sex, money, or because we don't want to feel alone. Don't stay with someone or fear leaving a bad situation for those toxic reasons. If you have to leave someone, then do it. It is not easy, but you can trust and believe it does get easier with time. When you create a bond with anyone, leaving is never simple. We all are humans with feelings, but your mind has to be stronger than your emotions. Feelings can get us and keep us in situations we don't need to be in, especially in romantic relationships.

First know who you are, what you want, and what you expect of yourself before you involve someone else. When you are comfortable and confident in who you are and what you want, you can better understand the person you're interested in.

SIX
MARITAL HEALTH

Marriage should be a beautiful thing. Over the past few decades, times have changed, and some people have lost hope that they will ever be married. Marriage is not taken seriously anymore. Some people are even scared to get married. The divorce rate has skyrocketed.

Many of us grew up idolizing marriage, and idolizing something always makes it unattainable. Instead, we should honor marriage as God does. Marriage is supposed to be fun, difficult, rewarding, and a great investment. It comes with many challenges, temptations, and trials and errors.

Idolizing marriage makes you hunger for a perfect person's admiration. If you find someone you consider "perfect," you are willing to act beyond your conscience to be exactly like or close to what you're idolizing. You will eventually think and act like whatever you are worshiping. This can be extremely damaging to the mind, body, and soul.

Honoring your marriage, however, means you

have a significant respect for someone with incomparable worth. You take the time to genuinely value an imperfect person through any circumstance, making sure to remember your own value so you can better appreciate the good in what you are honoring.

HONOR, DON'T IDOLIZE

How movies, television, and social media represent marriage hasn't helped our idol problem in this modern age. We idolize the marriages of Hollywood couples, people in the movies, and even marriage itself as being an ultimate life goal. Famous people may share a luxurious vacation or a home with a million likes and a child, but these picture-perfect things can't give people genuinely happy or satisfied marriages.

We also idolize the marriages of earlier generations as well. This may confuse some people, but when we look at those couples, we see longevity. That's it. We see a seventy-year marriage as a number and idolize it. We don't see the hardships those couples might have faced or the pain and mistreatment they could have endured. Not all lengthy marriages are unhappy ones, however. Many couples who have been together for years upon years have had their ups and downs (like every marriage does), but they showed respect and honor to each other and their commitment when the trials and tribulations came.

Have you ever noticed when you compliment an older couple in a store or talk to someone who has been married for a long time, they tell you, "If only you knew what I've been through" or "Stay single while you're young. Don't get married yet. Just enjoy life."

Most marriages back then that lasted a long time dealt with a lack of mutual respect or healthy communication, depression, chronic infidelity, mental and physical abuse, and unwanted love. They might have married because a mother or father chose their spouse. Marriage standards and motivations back then were totally different. Back in the day, you were expected to stay in a marriage regardless of mistreatment or danger. You were taught to stick it out and make things work. Today, spouses refuse to put up with abuse, chronic infidelity, and unhappiness, and I love that about this generation. People today realize their worth, in part thanks to the baby boomers who raised them, and millennial parents are teaching their children (and themselves) to remember those lessons of self-worth. Self-worth in marriage must be acknowledged and practiced by both partners, and we must remain committed to teaching by example.

Many millennials are getting married at a young age, living their best life and waiting for "their person," or not wanting a relationship at all. None of these choices is wrong. Everyone else is scared of love and marriage, however, and that is the only dangerous ground.

Whatever you choose, take your time with getting married. If you are married and know for sure you need to exit the relationship, do not stay because of religious teachings, children, or because you're afraid of starting over and being alone. Do what is right for the long term.

But how do we do marriage right? The main problems people have in marriage are because of finances, being unequally yoked, infidelity, and depression. We must stop idolizing and start honoring ourselves, our self-worth, and our souls first so we may produce good fruits and honor someone else in a long-term commitment.

IDEAL MARRIAGE

Respect and reverence for marriage is scarce today. Marriage is a contract, a covenant, a decision. Don't confuse emotions and moods with a true-love commitment. You work to make the relationship work. It's rarely easy, and people are quick to quit when things get hard.

"I don't need a man!"

"I don't need a woman!"

Yes, but if you married them, you promised not to give up on that person unless staying brings more harm to both of you. Search for all the red flags before you make that commitment to avoid wasted time and hurt. Don't settle, but also don't be so quick to yell, "I don't need anyone."

God made man for woman and woman for man. The sexes balance each other out.

For men, the Bible says in Proverbs 18:22, "He who finds a wife finds a good thing and obtains favor from the LORD." Proverbs 31:10 also says, "An excellent wife who can find? She is far more precious than jewels." For women, it says in Genesis 2:18, "It is not good that the man should be alone; I will make him a helper fit for him." For both partners to understand, Genesis 2:24 says, "Therefore a man shall leave his father and his mother and hold fast to his wife, and they shall become one flesh."

Even though times have changed, God's Word

will always remain the same. The Bible says in 1 Corinthians 13:4–8, "Love is patient and kind; love does not envy or boast; it is not arrogant or rude. It does not insist on its own way; it is not irritable or resentful; it does not rejoice at wrongdoing, but rejoices with the truth. Love bears all things, believes all things, hopes all things, endures all things. Love never ends."

Love is not an emotion, but today people still choose to love only with their feelings. Real love isn't supposed to be that way. Love is an action. The true nature of the heart drives our actions and is not made up of temporary feelings but of permanent commitment.

We all will love many people in our lifetime. This does not mean we should marry each one or try to make something work that is not meant to be. You can love someone partially, but when marrying them, you need to love wholeheartedly. Loving someone wholeheartedly may be a challenge, so it's good to know *The Five Love Languages* by Gary D. Chapman.

Words of affirmation, acts of service, receiving gifts, quality time, and physical touch are the five languages of love. Words of affirmation is love with words. Acts of service is love with actions. Receiving gifts is love with generous giving or surprising—even free gifts, because you don't have to spend money to be generous. Quality time is love with spending or setting time aside for someone. Physical touch is love with physical contact. We can love someone with all our heart, but if the other person mistreats us and doesn't act in love and we stay, then this means we accept that they don't fully love us. We tell them with our actions that we're only worth that partial love.

In an ideal marriage, one person cannot love more than the other. You must be equally yoked to have a happy and healthy marriage. Being *equally yoked* is a biblical term that refers to two oxen carrying the weight of a plow or cart together, and if we apply it to our relationships and marriage, then we can understand the full concept. Being equally yoked means going in the same direction spiritually, in agreement. You want to agree on the essentials of your faith, because light and darkness don't mix.

Remember dating yourself? Before you get married, you must love and understand yourself first, because marriage is a big commitment. You are choosing to love one person for the rest of your life. When you make your vows, honor and respect them. You become one with that person. So before you marry, make sure you are truly in love with that person for all the right reasons. Make sure you are ready for the good times and, most importantly, the bad times. Do not marry if you feel pressured by people around you. Marriage doesn't require perfection (that's impossible), but make sure your love for that person is unconditional. When you stay ready, you don't have to get ready. This applies not only to marriage but also to your everyday life.

MARRIAGE ADVICE

A healthy marriage requires a healthy relationship with God, good communication, and recognition of boundaries.

FOCUS ON A HIGHER IDEAL IN YOUR MARRIAGE

To weather the challenges of marriage, both you and

your spouse must rely on a higher ideal. People are imperfect, and you will always disappoint each other, so remain committed to encouraging one another toward a greater good. For many people, that ideal is God, so I'll discuss this higher ideal in those terms.

Turn to God in all situations, especially in times of temptation. Talk to God about your problems, and when you feel alone, ask him to send someone you can truly trust to talk to. If you sense an emotional, physical, or spiritual disconnect in your marriage, pray and talk to your spouse about it.

The grass is greener where you water it. In your relationship with God, what are you feeding your mind? Are you reading the Bible? Seeking godly advice? What movies, music, and media are you consuming?

If you listen to music about having different women, guess what you're going to want?

If you always watch movies about cheating on your man, guess what you're going to do?

Finding a person you can really love and trust is rare. So when you find someone worth keeping, protect that relationship by investing in your relationship with God. Regardless of who you are, at some point in your marriage, you will fight temptation.

Ephesians 4:27 says, "And give no opportunity to the devil." When you neglect your relationship with God, you give the devil opportunity to destroy your marriage. Mark 14:38 says, "Watch and pray that you may not enter into temptation. The spirit indeed is willing, but the flesh is weak." In 1 Corinthians 10:13, Paul says, "No temptation has overtaken you that is not common to man. God is faithful, and he will not let you be tempted beyond your ability, but with the temptation he will also provide the way of escape, that you may be able to endure it."

The flesh (meaning our human will) is susceptible to temptation. Whenever you get married, but especially if you do so at a young age, make sure you're ready. Be willing to let your partying lifestyle go. Let the drinking and smoking go. Let all harmful habits go before you make that commitment.

How can you stay faithful and resist temptation when you're drunk at a party full of people who won't hold you accountable? Are you going to stand there looking at a brick wall? No! You're going to get your groove on. If you still want to go out to scenes like that, honor your partner by bringing them and abstaining from the activities that cause temptation. If you can't restrain yourself, avoid those activities when entering a relationship. Watch your environment and the people you hang around. Sometimes you have to distance yourself from friends or family to have a healthier relationship. You'll learn in life that most good things require sacrifice. You get to choose what (or who) is worth that sacrifice.

When you first meet someone, talk about your beliefs. Successful husbands and wives have the same beliefs and are equally committed to their faith. This is being equally yoked.

Let's say one spouse is a Christian and the other isn't. Mark 3:25 says, "And if a house is divided against itself, that house will not be able to stand." James 1:6 and 8 say, "But let him ask in faith, with no doubting, for the one who doubts [. . .] is a double-minded man, unstable in all his ways." So if one spouse believes and the other doesn't, this causes conflict in the marriage. The believing spouse will want to maintain their relationship with God—go to church, raise a family in church, celebrate holidays, and have a godly marriage. The nonbelieving person will want to pursue other things.

Are you following along? Stay awake. It's feeding time. Make sure you and your spouse want to grow in the Lord together so you can encourage each other in your marriage. Knowing the Lord personally is not the same as understanding him together. Together, spouses can discover community and spiritual growth when they attend a church full of genuine believers. You may have understanding or strength in one topic, and your spouse may have understanding or strength in a different topic, so you can teach one another. Proverbs 27:17 says, "Iron sharpens iron, and one man sharpens another." You help your mate and they help you.

As you grow in your faith and your relationship with God, you can apply the lessons to your marriage. If you're not married but want to be, work to better understand what you believe so you have that foundation of wisdom to add to your future marriage. When things go left, look to God on the right for the correct answers. Stay focused and resist temptation.

KEEP OTHER PEOPLE OUT OF YOUR RELATIONSHIP

Don't talk about your spouse's problems with your friends and family, and keep your complaints off social media. It's too easy to post your relationship's every fight or victory, and this can be detrimental to your relationship's health. Even your close family and friends don't need to know every I-told-you-so moment or eye-roll reaction to your spouse's annoying habits. Hurting people hurt people, so when you're feeling strong emotions, take it out on your journal or in productive conflict rather than broadcasting it to a spiteful world.

For example, say a friend or family member you love is going through a hard time and they are single. They may seem down and trying to reconcile with life and reclaim their joy. You and your spouse are also going through hard times, and you need someone to vent to, so you choose that person. They may not intentionally give you the wrong advice, but this can easily happen when you passionately describe your concerns to someone who doesn't understand your commitment.

"Leave them. You're going through too much already."

"They are probably cheating on you."

"Go look for someone else."

"Stop giving them attention."

"Just file for divorce if it happens again."

These words flow easily from your friend's mouth if they are hurt or not in the right state of mind. They can hurt you and your relationship if you take the wrong advice based on their current situation. Your friend is probably not intentionally trying to downplay your relationship or tear you down (though some people might be), but this is why you should keep others out of your relationship.

When you need to talk to someone about your relationship or marriage, start with your spouse! Take the initiative. Find a good day and set aside time to talk about what's going on in the relationship. Figure out what happened, why it happened, and what you can do to resolve the issue and keep it from happening again in the future. Don't simply patch a problem or brush it away. Make sure you both understand what's going on, how the other person feels, and why and how it needs to be fixed in the long term.

Some arguments reoccur—let's be real, a lot of them do—but next time you will know the steps to bypass previous mistakes and fix the problem together.

If talking to your partner doesn't necessarily fix the issue, then try talking to an objective married friend or family member. Women, never seek relationship advice from single women. Men, never seek relationship advice from single men. For heaven's sake, this is one of the worst things you can do. My dad taught me this at an early age. Although I didn't always listen, I learned that you must apply this wisdom if you want a strong and healthy relationship or marriage.

Stay away from the opposite sex when seeking advice. Some people may seem like they are giving you good advice when they are trying to replace your significant other. If you're talking to an opposite-sex friend constantly about your relationship problems, what makes you think they don't want to fill the emotional (and eventually physical) spot that belongs only to your spouse? Emotional entanglements happen before physical cheating. This can ruin your marriage or relationship. Be careful.

Many people naturally want to talk to their mother or father about marriage problems. But do your parents fall into the *objective* and *married* categories? Ninety-five percent of the time, your family has your best interest at heart and wants to protect you. But even if your parents have a healthy marriage, it's difficult for them to be objective.

Say you have three small arguments with your spouse. For example, you told your family your significant other does not clean up after themselves, they won't go to college, and they are distant. You could be reasonably mad at these things. Your family could give you good advice on what to do, suggesting strategies to help you talk to your spouse about your concerns, or they could tell you to fight back in a petty way or leave them.

The more you bring your marital concerns to your parents, the more they may dislike your spouse! Now your family feels a certain way about your significant other all because you told them things that direct communication with your partner could have easily addressed. To recover, you have to work hard to tell your family good things about your spouse more often. Marrying into a good family is extremely important, but it can take time to build a great bond with your spouse's family.

If your spouse won't talk and you don't have another safe person with whom to work through your marital issues, talk to your pastor or go to marriage counseling. Many people wince when they hear the words *counseling* or *therapy*. Going to counseling shows you are committed to your spouse and want to better yourself. The only thing that should matter is fixing your relationship. What everyone else thinks does not matter, because they are not the ones loving you, your spouse is. This is not to say that everyone believes the counseling method is wrong, because in actuality, most people are for it. But those who believe otherwise may view counseling in a negative way.

Be careful who you vent to, because a listening ear can always become a running mouth. Now ten other people know what's going on inside your marriage because you told the wrong person. When choosing someone to talk to, make sure they are objective, married, and trustworthy.

Strive to be this objective, trustworthy ear when your friends and family need relationship and marriage advice, because trust me, you are not the only one who will need a listening ear. You get what you give, so give generously whenever you can.

SUPPORT YOUR PARTNER

Learn to be a help to your spouse. You and your partner are each other's biggest support system. The goal of a support system is to create a reassuring, safe place for your partner to return to. Learning to communicate, accept criticism, and stay accountable lays a foundation for a healthy, happy, and God-honoring marriage.

Understanding is the ultimate goal of good communication. Two people can communicate, but that doesn't mean they comprehend each other. A small misunderstanding can lead to unnecessary arguments. Arguments can be time-consuming, tiresome, and stressful. You can avoid most unnecessary arguments if you take the time to properly communicate with one another.

When you talk to your spouse, what kind of tone do you use? Remember James 1:19? It says, "Know this, my beloved brothers: let every person be quick to hear, slow to speak, slow to anger." Applying this principle in conversation with your partner, children, other family, and friends can improve your everyday life and your marriage.

Words can be hurtful, and sometimes it can take

years to forgive a harmful statement. You might forget your angry words, but the recipient never will. Especially with your spouse, learn to communicate and speak when you are in a calm state of mind.

As you grow, you change. Both marriage partners will change many times over the years. Even though you should date yourself often to learn about who you're becoming, you may miss some qualities that aren't easy to see from the inside looking out. If your partner says (in love) that you need to work on something, take the feedback under consideration. Explore the reasons why you might act that way and adjust your behavior as needed.

Criticism is a form of communication. When we feel criticized, we can automatically go into defense mode. Examine what your partner is telling you and see if any truth is in it. What parts do you and don't you agree with? Discuss what you think is true and how you can address it. This way, you take ownership of your actions, listen to your partner, and choose to talk about self-improvement without arguing. Be okay with constructive criticism. Neither you nor your partner should bash each other. Things your partner can't change are truly better left unsaid, but learning to accept, consider, and implement change in response to criticism is a skill that enables you to support one another.

Keep friends of the opposite sex at arm's length. Having friends of the opposite sex and calling them your sibling or best friend is common nowadays. But be cautious when entering a long-term committed relationship or marriage. Your opposite-sex friendships can ruin your romantic relationships, and here's why. Most friendships start out innocently. Nice gestures, friendly hugs here and there, laughs.

You become emotionally close to the person. You text and call, and eventually you start hanging out one-on-one. Dangerous territory! To you, they may just be a friend. But to them, the friendship could be much more.

Now let's say you're in a marriage. You start having problems, so you text or call your opposite-sex friend for a laugh, for comfort, or to discuss the problems. Maybe you want some peaceful time, so you don't start a big argument with your spouse. Instead, you hang out with your friend.

With that, you're saying your marriage (and by association, your spouse) is not worth the discomfort of this fight. You're disrespecting yourself and your partner. You're using the opposite-sex friend as a buffer physically and mentally. How would you feel if every time your spouse spends time with you, their phone rang with calls from that particular friend? Or how would you feel if you're home or at work and your spouse is hanging out with the opposite-sex friend? Most times, people know this behavior is disrespectful, so they try to hide parts of the friendship from their spouse. Other times, one partner will flaunt their friendship as a power move. You're setting yourself up for an affair!

Even if your friend also works with you, choose to set boundaries to respect your spouse and protect your marriage. Some friendships may not be as sinister as they seem, but even still, be mindful of the other person. Let's say you and your partner are arguing nonstop and you repeatedly go hang out with your opposite-sex friend. You start hanging out more and more until this "friend" is satisfying you more emotionally (and perhaps physically with innocent hugs and laughs) than your spouse.

Intimacy increases, and then bam! Affair.

See how easily things like this can happen? It may hurt your partner and make them feel as if they are not good enough or you don't care about them anymore. I'm not saying you can't have friends of the opposite sex, but if you want to hang out, invite them on a double date or group activity. When having a phone conversation, keep it short and focused on the tasks. Include your significant other in these conversations at all times. Whether your marriage status is good or bad at the moment, the goal is to show your spouse you are committed to them.

SEX

Our discussion on marriage and relationships wouldn't be complete without talking about sex. This topic makes us all cringe. Why does the word *sex* make everyone stop and glance around the room? Millennials talk about sex a lot. Among our friends and even on social media, it's brought up in songs and conversations every day.

We must educate ourselves about sex because it is more than a word, feeling, or act. Because of their complexity, sexual relationships are ideally saved until marriage. Sex is a complex issue that requires comprehensive education.

Let's first talk about valuing ourselves. In 1 Corinthians 6:19, it says, "Or do you not know that your body is a temple of the Holy Spirit within you, whom you have from God? You are not your own [. . .]." This means God wants us to treat our bodies with respect.

Some of us were likely raised to believe sex is a bad thing. It is not. Sex is definitely a good thing, but just like any other area of life, you have to have boundaries and educate yourself. For some young people, sex is seen only as a pleasurable biological act, perhaps of oral stimulation or penetration. This view strips sex of its full emotional and spiritual elements, exploiting it. So why does the Bible talk about saving our bodies until marriage? When two bodies and their fluids come together, you are experiencing more than the act of sex—it's much deeper than a lot of people think. You are creating emotional attachments and soul ties and exchanging energies and spirits with another person.

Let's break down each of these words.

Attachments are feelings that bind us to a person, thing, cause, or ideal.

Soul ties are unconscious spiritual connections. They can be mutual or one-sided.

Energies are the efforts and attention you direct toward a particular aim.

Spirits are your nonphysical parts (soul) that are the seat of emotions and character.

Whether or not you want it (or know it), sex enhances an emotional bond between you and your partner. This means that casual sex creates unseen and unknown bonds and connections. It's also poor spiritual and physical hygiene to give your body to everyone.

Discussions like these apply strongly to both sexes. Have you ever had sex with someone, and a couple days or weeks later found yourself acting moody or oddly strange? You can pick up different attachments from other people, and nine times out of ten, it's from sex. When you have sex with someone, the spirits of everyone your partner ever slept with could now leach into you. So just because you haven't slept with your partner's previous partners physically does not mean you don't emotionally have a connection. Take this into consideration before having sex.

Sex also comes with a lot more than just energies and emotions. Sex also can bring forth children. As we all know, it only takes one time for a child to be conceived. Making children is a good thing, but be smart about it. Choose to be wise about when, where, and how to have sex.

Sex can also cause sexually transmitted diseases and infections. This topic is touched on in school curriculums, but not nearly enough. Some STDs and STIs can have a horrible, long-term impact on your body and your health. Until the 1990s, sexually transmitted diseases were called *venereal diseases*. STDs often begin as STIs. They spread from one person to another during vaginal, anal, and oral sex or other intimate physical contact. Without treatment, they can lead to serious health problems.

In some cases, STDs don't always cause symptoms, or they may only cause mild symptoms, which means it is possible to have an infection and not know it. If you are having sex, get tested every time you change sex partners. Don't feel embarrassed to go or return to a clinic or doctor. Give yourself a pat on the back for being responsible and safely concerned about your health. I've listed some of the most common STDs and STIs and their symptoms and causes here:

Bacterial Vaginosis (BV)
Bacteria
A common vaginal infection that occurs due to a change in pH balance.
Symptoms: Foul-smelling, "fishy" vaginal odor. Vaginal itching. Burning during urination. Thin white, gray, or green discharge.

Chlamydia
Bacteria
STD caused by a bacterial infection.
Symptoms: Abnormal vaginal or penile discharge. Burning during urination. Pain and swelling in one or both testicles (less common).

Gonorrhea
Bacteria
STD caused by a bacterial infection. Often doesn't have symptoms.
Symptoms: Pain or burning during urination. Abnormal yellowish or bloody vaginal discharge or yellow, white, or green penile discharge. Bleeding between periods. Throat pain (for oral gonorrhea). Anal itching or discharge.

Herpes Simplex Virus (HSV)
Virus
Infection of the mouth and/or genitals that causes blistery sores. No cure, but symptoms are treatable.
Symptoms: Itchy or painful blisters on the vagina, vulva, cervix, penis, butt, anus, or on the inside of the thighs. The blisters break and turn into sores. Burning during urination if urine touches the herpes sores.

Hepatitis A, B, C
Virus
Virus that can cause liver disease. Spread through sex or sharing personal hygiene items like razors or toothbrushes.
Symptoms: Yellow skin or eyes (jaundice). Nausea. Abdominal pain. Fatigue. Fever. Some cases have no symptoms.

Human Immunodeficiency Virus (HIV)
Virus
Infection that breaks down the immune system and can lead to AIDS. No cure, but treatment can help an infected person stay healthy.
Symptoms: Abdominal pain. Pain or difficulty while swallowing. Dry cough. Fatigue. Fever. Loss of appetite. Malaise. Night sweats or sweating. Nausea. Persistent diarrhea. Vomiting or watery diarrhea. Sores or swelling in the groin. Mouth ulcers or white tongue. Coinfection. Headaches. Oral thrush. Pneumonia. Red blotches. Severe, unintentional weight loss. Skin rash. Swollen lymph nodes.

Human Papillomavirus (HPV)
Virus
Growths on the genital area and around the anus.
Symptoms: Vaginal discharge. Itching. Bleeding. Burning. Fleshy, painless growths (warts) on skin.

Scabies
Parasite
Tiny parasites that cause itching. Passed through skin-to-skin contact.
Symptoms: Intense itching where the mites burrow. Bumps or redness.

Syphilis
Bacteria
Infection causing ulcer sores at the first two stages and heart, brain, and other problems in the third stage.
Symptoms: Sores called *chancres*. Rash on the palms and soles. Painless ulcers. Vaginal discharge. Wart-like growths on genitals. Fatigue. Itching. Mouth ulcers. Sore throat. Swollen lymph nodes. Weight loss. Rectal lining inflammation.

Trichomoniasis "Trich"
Parasite
Major cause of vaginitis. Easily treated.
Symptoms: White, gray, yellow, or green and frothy vaginal discharge with an unpleasant smell. Vaginal spotting or bleeding. Genital burning or itching and redness or swelling. Frequent urge to urinate. Pain during urination or sexual intercourse.

Pubic Lice (Crabs)
Parasite
Small parasites that attach to the skin and hair near the genitals.
Symptoms: Intense genital itching. Tiny bugs in pubic hair. Crab eggs (which are called nits) at the base of pubic hairs. Dark or bluish spots on the skin where pubic lice are living. Fever. Fatigue. Irritation.

Yeast Infection
Fungus
Inflammation, intense itchiness, and a thick, white vaginal discharge.
Symptoms: Itching and irritation in the vagina and vulva. Burning during urination or sexual intercourse. Redness and swelling of the vulva. Vaginal pain and soreness. Vaginal rash. Thick, white, odor-free vaginal discharge with a cottage cheese appearance. Watery vaginal discharge.

You can always go to a doctor or contact a health care provider with any questions and concerns if you notice any symptoms. Don't be ashamed to talk to someone about your health. Some STDs and STIs are more serious when left untreated and also could affect pregnancies. Pay attention to your body so you can detect things right away when something is off. Educate yourself about your body as a whole, especially if you are sexually active.

Feed your mind.

SEVEN
OTHER THINGS WE SHOULD KNOW

Let's talk about some more useful things millennials and younger generations can apply to our lives to better ourselves and help others do the same. We can break the generational curse upon us and embrace a new generational chapter.

PHONE ETIQUETTE

Use polite phone etiquette. Answer the phone promptly within three rings, whether it is your personal phone or business phone. Immediately introduce yourself to the other person on the line. Speak clearly and in a pleasant tone. No one wants to struggle to hear someone with an inaudible, mumbly voice. We love talking on speaker phone. Do not do this unless it is absolutely necessary. Not everyone needs to be in on the conversation, and speaker phone causes too much background noise, which can be distracting. Use proper language when on the phone and remain cheerful and calm in conversation. Inject confidence into your voice!

Some younger callers are quick to say, "Hold on, I'll be right back," while they jump to put someone else on the call. Never do this. Always ask before putting someone on hold or transferring or joining a call. Last but not least, check and respond to voicemails. You may think voicemails are annoying, but get in the habit of listening to them. A voicemail informs you of why the call was made and also shows you are serious and responsible enough to respond to something simple. Leaving a voicemail does the same thing. It shows you are serious and confident enough to leave a voice message and would like a return call.

In this day and age, we are quick to hang up or text if someone does not answer the phone.

"Hey, I called you."

Okay? For what? Be detailed. Be professional. Do this on a regular basis. It helps you as an individual and prepares you to talk with business professionals when taking on a new job. Present yourself well. To project your voice well when you are speaking, sit up in your chair or stand. If you may forget things, write them down and rehearse them before you place the call. There's no room for unnecessary silence.

HANDSHAKES

In American culture, we use a handshake when meeting or greeting, completing a transaction, or expressing gratitude. Handshakes can also be a sign of good sportsmanship. Hand shaking conveys trust, respect, balance, and equality. When you shake hands with someone, always have a firm, strong grip. Don't shake too hard or too soft. While reaching to shake someone's hand, always make direct eye contact. This shows the other person you are serious. A weak handshake can indicate uncertainty or discomfort. You always want to show signs of confidence and seriousness. This is especially great in business and with friends and family, at events, interviews, and when casually meeting someone. You never know how far a balanced handshake can take you. Get in the habit of practicing this and it will become second nature.

CONVERSATIONAL ETIQUETTE

Good manners are great to add into everyday conversations. Let's go over some basics. Address adults by *Mr.* or *Mrs.* or *Miss*. Use the following words when you speak to someone you don't know well:

Yes, sir.
No, sir.
Yes, ma'am.
No, ma'am.

When trying to get someone's attention or asking for a response, you can say, "Sir?" or "Ma'am?"

Say "please" and "thank you" when asking or receiving.

When someone thanks you, in response, say, "You're welcome."

When asking, say, "Please may I?"

When engaging in conversation with a peer, avoid simultaneously emailing, texting, or talking on the phone with someone else. It is considered disrespectful.

Be an active listener by nodding or casually

saying, "Yes, I agree" or "Yes, I understand." Make eye contact during conversation.

Avoid words like *um*, *hmm*, *yeah*, and *mm-hmm* in conversations.

Pause and think before you speak, and when you do, use a measured pace. Avoid speaking rapidly, because you might say things you don't mean, and you may seem as if you don't know what you are talking about.

OLD-FASHIONED MANNERS

Some old-fashioned etiquette should be passed on. Many of the manners taught decades ago still apply today. These acts simply show respect and delicacy toward yourself and others.

Keep your elbows off the table when eating.

Take your hat off when inside a building.

Do not spit when you talk. Chew with your mouth closed.

Sit up straight and have good posture.

Always hold the door for others. Men, open the door for your lady, even the car door. It shows you are a gentleman. Ladies, hold the door for friends and family. Most of the time we open the door and put our hand back so another person can grab the door next. Simply get behind and hold a door, especially for elders. Do this for every person you can.

Use proper etiquette when eating. Most people do not know the proper way to hold a fork and cut with a knife at the same time.

Write thank-you notes instead of texting them. This shows you put time and effort toward thanking someone else.

Stand when greeting someone.

Cover your mouth when you sneeze or cough.

Wait to eat until everyone is served. Some parents let the kids eat first, and some eat whenever. In earlier generations, no one ate until everyone had their plate and after prayer was said.

Knock on a door before entering.

Don't reach across the table. Ask if someone can pass whatever you need.

Ask to be excused from the table.

Place a napkin in your lap while eating.

Spit out gum before you talk.

Wash your hands before touching food.

Offer help when you can give assistance, especially when attending someone else's function or gathering. Ask if they need help cleaning or offer to wash dishes. It may seem overbearing to some, but this small gesture can go a long way.

Times have changed, but some manners are still applicable.

PROFESSIONAL ETIQUETTE

Have you ever applied for jobs over and over and you can't seem to get the employers' attention? Or have you ever had back-to-back interviews and you never got a call back or a job offer?

If so, let's change that.

Rarely do any of us have someone explain the importance of creating a resume or preparing for an interview. Where you live could also play a major role in your job search or career. Living in a small town can be different from living in a larger city where more people compete for jobs.

Competition in the job market is huge, so learning how to present yourself well to hiring managers and companies will help you land and keep jobs.

Let's start with your resume. Everything from font size and type to layout says something about you. Employers have a myriad of resumes to look over, so they only spend a certain amount of time scanning each one. This means you want yours to be neat, easy to read, and to the point. Don't overdo or underdo it. Make it short. This includes the summary and your experience descriptions.

In professional resumes, employers look for simple fonts like Arial or Times New Roman. Keep your font sizes between ten and twelve points. This keeps your resume readable. Remember, the goal is to stand out. Look for a great template. You can usually go online and find great resume templates to use.

Now let's jump over to your interview call itself. (Speak love, joy, and prosperity over your life. Speak it into existence.) When an interviewer calls you, try to eliminate as much background noise as possible and speak clearly. Remember proper phone etiquette?

You never know who is calling you, so practice these qualities and apply them to your everyday life. Even though it may be a thirty-second call to set up a time and date, always remain professional. Jobs will sometimes do a phone interview before a face-to-face interview, so the same rules apply. When you have an in-person interview date set up and you're days away, prepare yourself.

Let's start with attire. How do you want to be viewed? This will affect your choices.

Ladies, a suit with heels or a dress is always a professional look. Your dress or skirt shouldn't be extremely tight or too short. If you decide to wear a dress or skirt with a blazer, don't wear super tall heels. You want to look like you are respecting yourself and the company. Keep your nails trimmed and clean at all times. Your makeup and hair should not look like you are going to a bar or club. Pull your hair back or, if you are wearing it down, keep it clean. Your makeup should be simple and jewelry should be kept to a minimum. A nice necklace and a pair of small earrings are fine.

For men, a suit is always professional. If the interview doesn't call for a suit, slacks with a shirt and tie or a button-down with dress shoes will do. Make sure your hair is cut well and your facial hair is neatly trimmed and groomed.

For both ladies and gentlemen, always iron your clothes. Don't show up to an interview in a wrinkled outfit. You don't have to spend hundreds on interview clothing. Bargain shopping can still find you reliable clothing at a reasonable price.

When you have your clothes ready, put them on at home and do a mock interview. Have a friend or family member be the interviewer or practice in the mirror. Make sure to practice with your full attire, makeup, and hair ready to go. Especially if you're really nervous or applying to big companies, practicing will benefit you. For your mock interview, use the STAR method. STAR stands for Situation, Task, Action, Result.

When answering behavioral and situational questions like "tell me about a time when" or "describe a situation where," use this method. Take the questions the interviewer asks and explain a situation you have encountered, a task you had, and the action you took to handle the situation, ending with a positive result. Keep it short and simple.

Few people know how to answer these questions well, so practicing will help you look more professional and prepared. The wording of some questions can seem a little tricky, but if you go over them beforehand, you will overcome your fears of answering these types of questions and have more confidence during your interview. Confidence is key when applying for jobs.

In no time, with practice, you will build confidence and be a pro at interviews.

Feed your mind.

EIGHT
POLITICAL HEALTH

You're probably thinking, "Why is it important for millennials to know about politics?"

Perhaps you've heard people say, "I don't really get into politics" or "I stay out of the way and don't pay attention to those things." But politics affects your everyday life. So educate yourself on the things going on around you.

What does the term *politics* mean? According to Merriam-Webster, politics is "the art or science of government," "concerned with guiding or influencing governmental policy," or "winning and holding control over a government." Politics is how groups of people make decisions—the rules and laws of countries and societies.

So how does politics affect our everyday life? We all need transportation, right? We all drive or ride on highways and interstates. We all need food to survive. We need a place to stay. We need to be informed about how we are taxed. We need fresh, clean, and safe water. When we use the internet, are we protected from scams and hacks? When we fly on airplanes or take cruises, are there safety guidelines and rules and regulations? What do we or our children learn in school? When we need a job, are there programs to help? When we own a house, what do our property taxes help pay for? If we rent an apartment, do we have rights if anything goes wrong? If we go to a park, who keeps the area clean and safe?

Politics is a broad term describing the actions of governments that affect our daily lives. When the government makes changes, it affects everyone, no matter our status. It influences what we can say and do in our workplaces and even sets the speed limits on the roads we use. Politicians are the people who practice in the field of politics and generally define the laws governing society. Politicians are generally elected by public vote and make up the legislative body of government. This is why your vote matters, and we millennials need to have a voice. When you don't vote, you are letting someone else make choices for you. According to a CNN article by Hunter Schwarz, millennials make up about 22 percent of the US population, and in 2020, they surpassed baby boomers as America's largest living generation.

We are a massive voting block and have the power to create change if we take a moment to educate ourselves. Wake up, millennials! Feed your mind! Educate it. Schwarz also quoted:

> "Millennials are drawn into politics over issues that affect them, like student debt, the economy, the environment, and health care," said Erin Loos Cutraro founder of She Should Run, a nonpartisan group that helps women run for office.
>
> "Millennials especially want to put their time

toward something they know they can change," she said.

Cutraro called millennials a "sharing generation" and said their comfort with social media could reshape politics, showing voters a different side of campaigning and lawmaking.

We have the voice, the power, and the brains. Use your brain and stop letting it go to waste. Do more research on politics, watch the news, or keep up with the stock market. If you are financially stable, you can even invest in stocks. Get educated about what affects your life.

Feed your mind.

NINE
NOTE TO SELF

Remember you are growing, not grown. You don't have the answers to everything, and you may never know why some things happen.

All we know is that life is life. And even with the chaos in the world, your friendships and relationships, and your home, life is still an amazingly beautiful thing, and good times and bad times are both a blessing. Be easy on yourself at all times, because you are all you have in the end. You may want to give up, but don't. Someone you don't even know is praying and rooting for you. Value your life, protect your peace, love hard, remain humble, and strive to do good.

Sometimes people take advantage of your compassion, and it may become tiring. I get it. Trust me, I was there. But always remain committed to do good and have a kind spirit, because those kinds of people are rare, and everyone you encounter and interact with will remember the beautiful soul you have. Keep pushing yourself and fight, even through your darkest days. Expect heartbreak and to feel sometimes like you don't want to be where you are. Expect the worst, but always prepare for the best. Better days will come.

Manifest what you want out of this life. Do not spend one second wasting time. This is your life. Make it count. Speak life over yourself. Proverbs 18:21 says, "Death and life are in the power of the tongue, and those who love it will eat its fruits." Stop lying to yourself about who you are and what you want! What you speak has power. Write down what you want out of life, because that is the first step to manifesting your goals. Habakkuk 2:2–3 says, "Write the vision; make it plain on tablets, so he may run who reads it. For still the vision awaits its appointed time; it hastens to the end—it will not lie. If it seems slow, wait for it; it will surely come; it will not delay."

When things aren't coming to you when you feel you deserve or want them, you must wait. Patience enables you to take advantage of opportunities as they arise. Matthew 7:7 says, "Ask, and it will be given to you; seek, and you will find; knock, and it will be opened to you."

Do you trust God when he's not "on time"? His timing doesn't always match ours, so remain watchful! You might miss your opportunity because it didn't arrive on your schedule.

Be mindful and pay attention to what the Bible says. When you apply these Scriptures to your life, they make sense. Understand all you can and be educated on as many things as possible. Be open-minded and willing to learn. Listen to constructive criticism. You are not perfect, and remember, you are growing every day. Do not get mad when someone tells you about yourself. If they want the best for you, they will apply loving pressure when needed and look out for you. This includes telling you when you are in the wrong or should change something. Don't be so quick-tempered. Sometimes the truth hurts, but it's beneficial to us overall.

Maintain your relationship with God, as he will guide you through life. Pray and have faith. Faith without works is dead. Why only pray and expect to get what you want or see results? You have to do more than pray. Have faith and believe. Be obedient to God's commands.

Stop playing around with your life. Be honest with yourself and with others. We are taught by today's culture to return evil for evil, sleep around, betray our friends, and the list goes on. Stay true to yourself and stop believing everything you see online. There's a saying: "Believe half of what you see, and none of what you hear."

If you have to give too much energy to someone and they are not showing equal effort, talk to them about the situation, because they may need help to realize. After that first time talking, if nothing changes, let the relationship go, and always remember that people who care about you most will make the greatest effort for you when the right time comes.

Similarly, you have to get up and make some effort to get results. Don't expect a cheesecake to appear on your table if you don't buy the ingredients, look up a recipe, and make it. We have to stop being lazy. You are beautiful ladies and handsome fellas. Tell this to someone you know and a stranger each day, because you never know what kind words and small gestures can do for another person. Be realistic and spread love, peace, and prosperity.

This world needs you. And most importantly, *you* need you. The better version of you.

I love you, God loves you, and you should love you.

When you achieve success, keep striving for ways to better your relationships and investments. Keep feeding, display good fruits, and you will harvest more than you can imagine. You're awake. Your mind is now fed. The rest is up to you.

REFERENCES

Anxiety & Depression Association of America. "Understanding Disorders: What is Anxiety and Depression?" Accessed May 27, 2021. https://adaa.org/understanding-anxiety.

Chapman, Gary D. *The Five Love Languages: How to Express Heartfelt Commitment to Your Mate.* Chicago: Northfield Publishing, 1992.

Fox, Maggie. "Women Twice as Likely as Men to Have Depression, Survey Finds." NBCUniversal News Group. Updated February 14, 2018. https://www.nbcnews.com/health/health-news/women-twice-likely-men-have-depression-survey-finds-n847556.

Galov, Nick. "Latest Social Media Marketing Statistics in 2020." Review42. Updated November 16, 2021. https://review42.com/resources/social-media-marketing-statistics.

Gilchrist, Jacqueline. "Dave Ramsey Baby Steps List: How to Manage These 7 Financial Steps." Mom Money Map. February 2, 2021. https://mommoneymap.com/dave-ramsey-baby-steps-list.

Mental Health America. "Suicide." Accessed May 28, 2021. https://www.mhanational.org/conditions/suicide.

Merriam-Webster Collegiate Dictionary, 11th ed., s.v. "politics." Accessed May 28, 2021. https://www.merriam-webster.com/dictionary/politics.

Ross, Mathew. "Suicide Among College Students." *American Journal of Psychiatry* 126, no. 2 (April 2006): 220–225. https://doi.org/10.1176/ajp.126.2.220.

Schwarz, Hunter. "How Millennials Could Kill Politics as We Know It If They Cared To." *CNN Politics.* October 8, 2018. https://www.cnn.com/2018/10/07/politics/how-millennials-could-kill-politics-as-we-know-it/index.html.

Sinrich, Jenn. "6 Ways That Social Media Has Changed Health and Fitness." Aaptiv. June 21, 2019. https://aaptiv.com/magazine/social-media-fitness.

Solo Traveler. "Solo Travel Statistics and Data: 2020." November 10, 2020. https://solotravelerworld.com/about/solo-travel-statistics-data.

The Checkup. "Depression Statistics 2021." Updated January 21, 2021. https://www.singlecare.com/blog/news/depression-statistics.

Made in the USA
Columbia, SC
19 November 2024